SAGA

SAGA

Hannah Mettner

TE HERENGA WAKA
UNIVERSITY PRESS

Te Herenga Waka University Press
Victoria University of Wellington
PO Box 600 Wellington
teherengawakapress.co.nz

A catalogue record is available at the National Library of New Zealand

ISBN 9781776921157

Printed in Singapore by Markono Print Media Pte Ltd

for the hags

Contents

Everything that ever happened to me
is just hanging—crushed
and sparkling—in the air

—Mary Ruefle, 'Saga'

Saga

In the tradition of my people, I come to you
with a long and winding story that neither
starts at the beginning nor finishes at the end.
There is, however, a lot of middle, which is
the way with all the best sandwiches. I mean
sagas. In the tradition of my people, I'm often
distracted by food, but that is only my body
doing its best to keep me alive. Strange that
I have grown up to become neither a folk hero
nor a king. Instead, I am a woman who pickles
vegetables. I have the stained fingers of a
person who knows arcane secrets, and is not
afraid to share them. Like my ancestors, the
secret to my existence is buried under the
permafrost, which is set to melt any day now
and bring enlightenment to us all. My gut
feeling is that we won't like what we discover
and will wish to put things back to how
they were. Which we all know is
impossible.

In the language of this country, I learn to say
that my ancestors come from the fjords.
A place I've never visited, but imagine to be
exactly the right temperature for my fickle
body. A place where I could look like the woman
from the Timotei ad, shaking my long hair out
under a waterfall. A place where I am never
too tall. There, I would joyfully hand in my
organzas to become a devotee of the traditional folk
costume of my ancestral seat. And the language

might choke me slightly as I swallow it down
in great mouthfuls, the shop-people tendering
their responses in polite English, but I will know
what I mean, which is more than I can usually say
for myself. It's funny how slippery the idea of home is
if you spend any time thinking about it.
And how no one asks white people that terrible
question, where are you from, even when they're
the absolute furthest away from where they
started.

In the interests of historical accuracy, I should
let it be known once and for all that the family
recipe is a dud. The recipe is for a pineapple
cheesecake made with evaporated milk and no
cream cheese whatsoever. I guess it's true that
some people just don't want to enjoy life. I learn
too that I belong to the 'crying side' of the family
and that the mythos of the non-crying side
circles like wolves round a fire, coming in close
to tear the limb from a sleeping cousin before
loping back into the night. My aunt reports
that we used to be Vikings, but it is clear that
that was a very long time ago. For example
all my hobbies are activities that involve sitting
down and not being killed. I only learn these
things as I learn that it is rude to introduce
myself with nothing more to offer than a name.
My history tightens around me like a knot and
there is wild blackberry growing through it
like everything here.

Autobiography of a Riot Grrrl

I am a girl, spending my girlhood learning
about men.

Anyway, this is the only education there is, and I am lucky
to have it. I think like this—what not to do—
what to do better—
putting the past behind me like the last tree falling
in the dark forest that has separated us
all these superstitious centuries.

I walk out, swinging the axe.

                   I unbutton myself
for bed and find the tough heart of a man clenched
beneath the hot silk
of my skin.

I can feel it
                   pressing up behind my teeth
like feelings. My heart wants many things—wants
to be many things—
a dealer in antiques—a navigator—painter—
professor—philosopher—
god
forbid it
a poet

Birth control

We begin with the viral video of the anaconda
in New England giving birth to her exact genetic copies
because she's never even *seen* a male snake
in all her eight years behind glass.

The headlines are calling it a virgin birth.

I watched the video this morning—
now everywhere I turn, a Madonna, a snake.
Oh, Rome, how you worship your silk-hipped mothers!

You heap your offerings of smoke and ash, your hard heels
of bread. This church is just another *Santa Maria*
with an old woman in a shawl
shaking a takeaway coffee cup outside.

*

At the Vatican, I wonder
if he-who-sees-everything can see the small T-shaped
thing inside me. I walk through the metal detectors and bag check
and have the surreal thought that the Pope
might sweep down to deny me entry
like Jesus in *The Last Judgment*.

When I first had it inserted, I bled for a month
and ruined all the underwear I owned, even
though I rinsed them in cold water first
the way my mother taught me.
Every day I'd think it'd stopped, but it kept coming—
Mary's stigmata, Eve's—relentless

like the blood after birth—
uterus closing like a fist
with nails cutting into the palm.

In the Vatican there is so much art, so much wealth,
but what I notice is the absence of Madonnas.
Every wall in Rome is frescoed with Marys
except here, the holy centre.

*

At home, my daughter, who has grown
so tall so quickly it looks like someone has grabbed her
at either end and pulled, starts taking the pill
to manage her bleeding.

Six months ago she was innocent as grass.
Seems like every initiation into womanhood is an initiation
into pain. Into seeing the other women
busying around us, bruising hips
on the corners of tables, gasping
in the bathroom as their stitches tear—
trying to hold back the knowledge of it, doing their best
always, always rubbing honey into the wound, almond
butter into the cracks in their hands, delivering us
into the knowledge of blood.

*

In this church the colours are fairy floss and hayfever
and bubble-gum-flavoured milk but Byzantine.

The gold is so bright that we glow a bit, and joke

about burning up as we walk in. If God made gold, it was
definitely for this—to dazzle us into a submissive kind of belief.

But, later, all these churches later, what I'll remember
is the fresco of the one woman with her arms held wide
trying to call her companions
to order, like *Bitches, please,*
and that poor woman
on her left with a toddler *and* a baby on her lap
each clamouring for a breast.
Another woman seems to be resting a sandalled foot
casually on the decapitated head of a man. Her robe
drapes a bit in the blood, but she's too deep in conversation
to notice that. On the far side of the group
the woman in blue has her arm raised
to receive a raven while she whispers in her friend's ear.

This is the pastel chaos of womanhood. And behind them
all in black, a neat semicircle of men.

*

What's helpful is to know what 'Blessed be
the fruit' actually means. It's what the serpent said to Eve
just before she bit—what Eve said
to Adam, juice dripping down her chin.

*

In Rome, outside every church are four or five
armed soldiers and a jeep, spilling ash from their cigarettes
onto the cobblestones, watching. Kitset boys in camouflage
and blood-red berets.

I sit on the steps of the fountain and google the church—
the first church in Rome dedicated to Mary, it holds the head
of the virgin martyr Saint Apollonia. But before that
it was a pagan temple dedicated to Carmenta—
goddess of childbirth, prophecy and technical innovation.
Inventor of the Latin alphabet.

And the old woman, begging outside? One of the soldiers
calls her Maria and hands her a bombolone
wrapped in a paper napkin.

*

The light around the broken temple of the virgins
is orange and thick. If the flame went out, the women
were blamed for being unchaste. Whoever the culprit—
she was buried alive with just enough apricots and milk
to make the death a low-angled wasting. What would her heart
do, while her face was pulling back into its bones?
She would cry, and you would too, for spending your life
a servant to fire, and never knowing
how it felt to burn.

*

Parthenogenesis is the ancient word for a virgin birth—
not magic, but a well-documented biological process
in many plants and animals. Typically, what has happened
is that if men can't explain a thing, they call it witchcraft
and destroy it. There is a hymn for everything here
and this is the hymn for days made narrow through lack
of sleep. This is the hymn for the good–bad gift
of knowing.

Turned on by storms

Before they had the world explained to them, our ancestors
believed that storms were caused by the gods fighting, but
did they ever consider the gods fucking—the racket they'd make.
As if the whole world wasn't watching.

We are walking, pulled into the evening by the itch of something
happening. The wind rising to swallow the civet odour
of an overripe summer. The moon snuffed and steaming
under a pile of damp clouds.

Lightning flickers like a television left on in another room.
We keep turning, too slow to see the show till at last it breaks loose
over the scrubby silhouette of the hills—
the full drama of weather.

And we break loose then too, running, shrieking like teenagers—
kissing under the wooden fort by the sports field
with our hands inside one another's clothes.
This could be the last fort of its era

which is also my era—could be my last chance to play
on a playground that was around during my childhood.
What is this feeling of being old and young at the same time—
of living and dying, oh, all at once?

A small man is running laps—one fast, one slow—
his headlamp lighting us up then eclipsing us. He seems
completely unaware of what's happening overhead
and over here—my feet soaking in my lilac Chuck Taylors and my face hot

and the sky pulsing like a thin skin over the busy organ of the universe.
Everything around us charged and charging, and us the spark
which sets it all alight. And this is how I know that we are gods too—
at least for tonight.

Praying the gay away

The function of prayer is not to influence God,
but rather to change the nature of the one who prays.
Well, Kierkegaard said that, and I wanted to believe
him, the way I believed everyone smarter than me.

For so long, I prayed without mentioning it—
opening each address with *Dear God* like a blasphemy—
the prayer's omission a pill of salt on my tongue.

But God is a drug dog. He sniffs you out. He knew.
And he knew that I knew that he knew. And he's never
lost a staring contest, not once in all these years—
of course I was the first to look away.

That's how prayer turned to bargaining, and the balance
of power between us has been off ever since.
Always on my knees, bartering myself for a miracle.

The worst of it was that I loved church—
the outside-of-real-life-ness of it. The milk and honey of it.
The little plastic shot glass of Ribena and neatly squared
tablets of white bread that I would press into a bullet to eat.

The long sermons that I could always guess the end to.
Predictable how often someone was going straight to Hell—
That's me, I would think, sweating through my good dress.
Stroking my shame like a dog as it turned to me
with trusting eyes.

The central paradox of my existence—God didn't
make mistakes, but he made me. My anger grew legs—

ran away, dipped a toe into a lake of flame and found it
actually quite nice. Better than a jacuzzi on a cold night—
not a bad place to just . . . stew for a bit.

You see, in the end, prayer is nothing
more than the writing of lines in chalk
on the soft black of your heart until
it is completely covered up.

Bury your queers

I was in my last year of high school when Tara died.
I didn't see it, but I heard about it the next day
from all my straight friends. A bullet, not even meant
for her, right through the heart. At least, they said, it was quick.
She didn't know she was dying. Of course, I thought, she
had to die. It was destined.

Back then, queer characters were all Chekhov's guns.
As soon as you saw two women smile at each other
across a Wicca circle at college, you knew, before the end
of the season, one of them would be dead.
Remember when we first saw each other
at the open mic night at the student bar?

I think I knew, even then, how it would end.
The fireworks and brimstone, the spray of my blood
across your shirt. I didn't know how to love gently—
the tragedy of us already glowing red in my breast.
Back then I'd never even seen a happily-ever-after—
I only knew it all going up in flames.

La bohème

Using your last few dollars to buy ink instead of food sounds like something those sad old guys—Baudelaire and stuff—would do. Shaking their skinny white fists at the bourgeoisie. Shaking with their need for another drink. It took me a while to learn that I was poor, and even longer to learn that it wasn't shameful. Starving in a garret in Paris in the late-eighteenth century is the romantic alternative to freezing in my overpriced flat in Aro Valley, where the wind brings the first snow of winter right into my chest. Being cold makes me feel poorer than I am, as if I haven't built an insulation of books and my grandmother's rug— the only inheritance I can hope for. The desperateness of just living is getting me down—always soaking lentils overnight because they're cheaper that way—always pulling another jersey on—how can I write in these conditions? I know I wouldn't spend my last few dollars on paint or ink. I'm the body of my brain, and I'm hungry. I meet up with my friends and we ask each other *are you writing*, and we shake our heads. *No, we all say, no, I'm working.* And art isn't work because it doesn't pay the rent. Sometimes I see all our unmade things following us around like a haunted parade—Van Gogh's unsold sunflowers springing up around us as we run for the bus in our professional clothes.

Guns, lots of guns

Nowadays, historians reckon van Gogh cut off his ear because he hoped it might stop the roar of his tinnitus, not because he was mad. I read this at three o'clock one morning when I am wondering whether a knitting needle or a fondue fork would be the better implement for stabbing into my ear. I've been calling on the ghosts of past sufferers—Darwin and Michelangelo and Beethoven. The martyrs and geniuses. *Well, you decided to be a poet,* Mum said on FaceTime earlier, *didn't you sign up for a life of misunderstood suffering?* She jokes in the tone she'd use when I was small, when I'd turn to Dad and ask, *Is she kidding?* Bob Dylan, Neil Young, Barbra Streisand. I can't imagine Babs lying awake in her curtained boudoir thinking dark thoughts about the noises in her head. She'd get up, in her flowing satin nightgown, take herself out to a grand piano in a courtyard full of fragrant night-flowers, and she would distract herself. Her two cloned dogs, trained never to yap, would sit on either side of her piano stool. It's Keanu I fixate on though. In an interview he says *It doesn't bother me anymore*, in the same deadpan way he says *Guns, lots of guns*, in *The Matrix* and then as John Wick. I revisit this possibility again and again like a rosary. My doctor tells me tinnitus is often brought on by stress, and I think of Keanu's tragedies—dead baby and dead wife, the specific horror of being memed. His blankness a kind of Zen. His face an icon of unconcern. In the blue light of my phone, it's easy to imagine myself as one of his heroines—easy to imagine his cool hands on either side of my face like bone idols on a dark altar, his forehead against my own. The world blazing past us in a hail of gunfire that we don't even hear over the sound of our hearts ringing in our ears.

Hold-up at the Sleepbank

I didn't have a single dream left in me—never made it far enough down that dark corridor. I kept withdrawing from the Sleepbank even though I'd been overdrawn since the baby years. One night I made my last stand. Now, most people would come in hot, cowboy-hatted and -booted, fringed vest swinging, shouting 'Stick em up!' Instead I disguised myself as the mother of young children, greying hair in a messy bun, sagging activewear. I slid a note to the teller. When she looked up, I showed her my gun. *Desperate times* I said. She didn't make a fuss, so I squished my overnight bag through the gap in the clear partition between us and told her to fill it up. When I got home, though, the dreams I'd stolen went off like dye bags through my sleep—the sex with my brother—the lost in a jungle with an anaconda around my throat—the colleagues laughing at me in the break room as my teeth fell from my face. I was tainted by them, haunted, as cup of coffee after cup of coffee slipped through my hands.

If not nuclear

Turns out no one knows what they're doing
    when they're a teenager, which is why
it's a terrible time to have a child. We didn't
    even know how to take care of ourselves—
taking ourselves grocery shopping like we
    were playing at being adults. Spending all
our money on cheese, forgetting bread
    and milk. The old ladies of the supermarket
rubbing my belly like a genie's lamp
    just to remember the lemon-barley
edge of adulthood.

When you came to us, eventually, you
    looked like a wise old monk, and I was
relieved. Now, I thought, she will tell us
    what she needs. And you did try—
you were so articulate—but we were not
    yet fluent in your language. I was finding
it so difficult—I had gone into that water bath
    barely a woman, and come out of it a mother
and child.

But—this is a difficult thing to admit—
    I thought it'd be easy. I didn't realise my
body would develop a chemical dependency
    on your every breath. My mum would tell
me sleep deprivation is the most effective
    form of torture, as if this should comfort me.
I was always crying, *Don't wake the baby*
    but you always woke. And if you didn't
I would hold my finger under

your tiny nose, waiting for
your hot exhalations, to reassure myself
    you hadn't died in your sleep.

Everything I've ever done with intent
    has been a mistake. Like the time I cut
off all my hair and saw how visible
    my face was. Like when I saw the shells
on the grass asking 'WILL U MARRY ME?'
    and I thought, *No, I cannot*, but I did.
Because what is a family
    if not nuclear?

Three times a cat lady

Everyone knows the Cat Lady trope
began with a witch and her familiar.

Some Middle Ages douchebag got upset
when she said she couldn't go back

to his place because she had to get home
to feed her cat and lo! word spread

that she had hexed his dick. First, they
whispered about her in the tavern, then

they laughed, then they threw slop at her
when she went to town to do the shopping.

And if half the townspeople were to die
that winter? She shrugs at the cat

as she spins wool—who's laughing now?
She has magic enough for her needs

but it is merely the magic of feeding
something and being loved by it in return—

the magic of putting a seed
in the ground and eating what it grows.

*

And that's not the half of it—because
of the hex there isn't a single man in town

who'll marry her. So she takes care of herself—
she's good at that—not for her a fear

of the dark—*she's* not too squeamish
to snap a chicken's neck for her supper.

She forgets it is a crime not to fulfil
the mandatory requirements of womanhood—

wife and mother, meek and smothered.
They keep leaving dying things

at her door as a test—if they live she'll
be punished for the magic of meddling

and if they die, they'll get her for murder.
She's been around long enough to know

their tricks. She does the arithmetic, she is
167 years old in cat years, and she feels it.

*

The Cat Lady has nine lives too. How else
do you think she survived the drowning

the burning the crimes of passion
the rough sex gone wrong the childbirth

the hysteria myth the male bias
in medical research the walking home

alone at night the systematic culling
of women over centuries?

Like the cat, the Cat Lady is not entirely
apex predator nor prey. She lives in a state

of fight or flight. And when she fights
she enjoys it. She toys with her prey—

she lets it think it might get away—
and then she bites off its head.

Single-woman gothic-horror

I have a friend who keeps her knives sharp.
Once, when I was visiting her, I cut a lemon

for our drinks, and took the tip of my finger
with it. As she found me a plaster she told me

they're not intended as a trap, and I believed
her, but I knew also that any man, slicing

tomatoes for toast the morning after, would not.
Losing blood like his dignity, she would not

comfort him, her voice like a distant mother
to a small child, *Oh dear, what have you done?!*

She told me, *I wouldn't describe myself as
a violent person at all, but I often dream*

*of gore. I wake from a fight with my hand
still curled round a knife.*

And I know what she means, I have planted
hellebores beneath every tree in my garden.

I'm not planning on poisoning anybody
but I take comfort knowing they're there.

In winter, they bloom so hard it's like
minimalism never happened. They bloom

like loathing, or paranoia, or dread.
They bloom like the dead.

Love poem with gratuitous sex

Outside, the pandemic
runs through its declensions. There is something
so old-fashioned about seeking sanctuary
from a plague, but there is, too, something
old-fashioned about you.

How you are always at confession, though your confessor
is not the church. You lick the first two fingers
of your right hand, and it is you who moans
as you press them inside me, mouth
muted against my breast.

Each day, I wake up somewhere imaginary
which is to say I wake up inside the shape of your arms.
The bright white of your linen sheet someone else's
erotica—the rain on the roof
an ancient mammalian nostalgia.

Japanese anemones gather in a blue and white
ceramic sake jar beside your bed. A single bee
is trapped inside and takes
asylum there, before you offer it
the window.

I would take a photo of you
breathing, just that, listening to the crickets
winnow the dusk down to darkness.
Your face is different when you're not looking
at me and I couldn't tell you which I prefer.

Breakup poem at Auckland Art Gallery Toi o Tāmaki

In the Grey Room at Auckland Art Gallery
I tell a woman I don't love her. I tell her via text

with Gretchen Albrecht's huge painting
of a cloud, a country, occupying my field of vision

completely. The wall behind the painting
isn't grey at all, but a dazzling, electric blue.

The same blue of Frida Kahlo's
Casa Azul, which my sisters are visiting—

sending me Snapchats of their faces filtered
with flower crowns and monobrows.

I *want* to love her, and I tell her this, but that
just makes it worse for both of us.

She is my ideal woman—she is my ideal woman
and she has red hair cut with a fringe, so why can't I

make myself tip into giddy for her?
What a cunt. Always getting in my own way.

Always striving for honesty but saying something
hurtful instead. The only other person

in the gallery is a young woman reading Anne Carson's
Autobiography of Red and ignoring the art—

that's the kind of book you see someone reading
and feel like you know them—

that they must feel the same split-open way you did
on reading it. The problem with me

and the ideal woman is that we like all the same books
but never for the same reasons—

like, we're always not quite in sync. The problem
with me and the ideal woman

is that we both value our mental health too much
to have the Frida and Diego,

Geryon and Herakles kind of love.
The problem with me is that I want that kind of love anyway.

Why am I like this—
is a question I try not to worry at too often

but I'm asking it now—why am I always putting aside
something good for the myth of something better?

This is a high-stakes way to break up—being psycho-
analysed via text in a terracotta-red room

with a thousand painted old people looking down at me
from their gold frames.

Because I don't want to hurt her feelings
and because I keep hoping *my* feelings might yet arrive

the conversation goes on too long. She's right—
I've done a bad job because I still want her to like me.

What I should've said, she says—
This isn't working. It's over.

The well of loneliness

It's difficult to read the book without developing the initial crush on Stephen—tall with her wavy chestnut hair cut short. Narrow-hipped and broad-shouldered. Looks good in a suit. I get the hots for her too quickly, which is a trap I often fall into. Except this time it's a well, not a trap. It's only once we're in the well together that I realise how boring she is, how self-pitying and miserable. I try to cheer her up but she doesn't laugh at any of my jokes. It's enough to make me want to drown in here, or drown her. Luckily, I'm a strong swimmer, even though I fear the thing that could sweep up from the depths at any moment and pull me down with it. What is that? To distract myself from the thing, I consider kissing her, just to see if it's any good. My interest in the book was in the scandal of it. But it turns out the only action she gets is a bedtime peck on the cheek. God, no wonder the book is so depressing, has she ever actually had a decent pash? I do it, and she clings to me with such desperation that I struggle to keep my head above water. Her mouth is hot and the kiss is good, almost good enough to forgive her Christ-complex and bad politics and the way she never shares her wealth with her friends. Almost good enough to finish the book. Instead, someone flings a rope ladder down and I step onto it and out of the water, just as the thing rises up, quick and dark, and gets her. Glug, glug, glug.

Anita

I know this—I'm the eldest daughter
of the eldest daughter. If I was a man
this would mean I had land, a secret

handshake. Would mean I had the kind of mind
that accesses memory like facts stored tidily
in small catalogue drawers, always able

to lay a hand on the benefit of the doubt.
But I'm a woman, and women have been thrifty
with their appearances on the record—

attending to the context of men, then—
blip, disappearing. *Try searching their husbands'
names*, the archivist suggests, *their sons'*.

The only way I find them is through
births, deaths and marriages.
They are not mapped to anything

that doesn't concern their bodies. I want
to know them in the moonlight—thinking.
Stepping outside is like diving into

a chlorine-bright pool where everything
is hard and modern and floating.
To give myself the gift of physicality, I open

a new lipstick standing in the undertow
of foot traffic on Lambton Quay, twisting
the square-ended tube to reveal a creamy

French nude—Anita. The crisp, unused point
of it emerging like the toe of a shoe
from under a full-length black gown.

Anita, by NARS, my everyday lip.
Anita—applied at my desk without the aid
of my selfie camera. Anita, who were you?

A ballet teacher full of quiet discipline?
A set designer for the theatre—pulling other worlds
into this one, briefly, then letting them ping back

through the meniscus, leaving
audiences astonished. The type of woman
who would never sweat. Anita—

the French version of my own too common
name—history looping back like overdone hair.
Unable to write—not even to let your parents know

you had made it here alive.
Anita—the Frenchwoman married to the
Norwegian whaler, sleeping with a rifle

and an axe under your bed when
he was away, and he was away a lot.
Did you sleep Anita, really, with your small

girl alongside, and then all of those sons?
Anita—did your thighs spackle beneath
your dress like mine, or were you

the bony hungry type? Anita—is that you crying
at the edge of a wild river remembering
the bridges back home? Anita—

with the fragrance from the under-layers
of your hair picked up and dispersed by the wind—
you are part animal here, part woman.

Could you have imagined
that 150 years later the Coca-Cola Company would be
bottling this river for sale? Anita—

I see you. Through the goose-egg glaze
of the mirror where I parse
my own reflection for some kind of meaning—
pressing my kiss onto folded tissue.

Driving lesson

We drive through the old cemetery
on the coldest day of summer. It smells
like smoke and clover, which are the smells
of camping near a river, but we are not
in that life.

I want to talk to you, really talk, while
we're spared the burden of facing each
other, but we drive past a man about my
age with two small children crying near a grave.

I thought this place was full, that there
weren't any recently bereaved to interrupt
as you learn the gears and manage your revs.
Somewhere, unseen, birds are crying their dark cries.
It feels like winter and I feel the most like a mother
I've ever felt—grappling for warmth, and silent.

Beep test

At school, the worst class was PE—
our twice-weekly lesson in sunburn
and body shame. And the worst part of PE
was the beep test. Our smirking teacher
would line us up against the wall of the gym
then she'd saunter back to the bleachers
and the old tape player. When it beeped, we ran.
The aim was to get to the opposite end
of the gym before the next beep.
We'd start slow, ambling as a group over
the scuffed outlines of a netball court, but the
beeps kept coming, faster and faster. Us slow
girls would drop out early, pink and breathing
hard and feeling stupid for even trying to keep up.
Soon the sporty girls and the competitive girls
would be sprinting back and forth so fast they'd
slam into the walls at either end. So fast
they'd warp the space–time continuum.
Every now and again a girl would fall from the
thicket, clutching a broken toe, bursting out
in bruises, but the beeps would keep coming.
And the girls, they would just keep running.

[BEEP]

Having a good job means our parents
can measure us against the kids we grew
up with and feel smug that they did a good job
raising us, patting us back into their wallets
like a big wad of cash saved up for later.
Having a good job is having an answer when

41

someone asks you what you *do*—every friend
of a friend you meet for the first time at the bar
before the gig, every date you meet after work.
But I don't want any of that—the carefully curated
LinkedIn page, the business card with my name
on it, the work phone with the sound always on—
the promotion. I just want some time to think
about things I'm not being paid to think.
I want to spend an entire week pulling weeds
from my garden and planting vegetables in their place.
The sun dropping freckles on my shoulders.
An entire year where I don't have to be somewhere
at a certain time, and no one is scheduling
another team-bonding exercise over lunch.

[BEEP]

I wish I could slough off my workday as easily
as make-up sweating from my face into the neck
of another dress with pockets. If I don't walk
home, I don't exercise—I go from sitting
at my desk, to sitting on the bus, to sitting
on my couch, noticing that no one on TV ever
watches TV. Waves of heat and brand fragrance
pour from the shops on Lambton Quay.
This is the modern version of running the gauntlet—
resisting the basic human urge to step into light
and warmth. What I don't need, this is the stuff
that gets me—a pair of sparkly shoes, a hair clip
shaped like an octopus, the heady gush of dopamine
as I lay my little card on the machine and it dings.
A reward, I tell myself, for another day. But we all know
there is no way to satisfy an addiction to a system

designed to entrap us. No matter how fast I run
I can never get away.

[BEEP]

In my performance and development meeting
I admit to my manager that I have no ambition.
I admit that I have no interest in being developed—
that I just want to do my job and go home.
My manager leans in and says she'll let me in
on a little secret. *That's what the performance
part of all this is*, she says. It's not enough to do
the job, I have to look like I enjoy doing the job
and want to keep doing it, better every year.
The performance of being a professional.
She suggests I think of my work self as an alter ego—
but my alter ego is a power dresser who has slept
her way to the top and enjoys long, boozy lunches.
My manager asks where I see myself a year from
now and I say can I think about it and come back
to her, but I know I will not.

[BEEP]

I apply for a new role at my current workplace which
I know I could do easily. The hiring manager calls
to let me know I was a close second, but that I didn't
get the job because I lack confidence. They give the job
to a straight white man who leaves after a month
and when the job is re-advertised I don't reapply—
mostly out of spite. I don't believe that confidence
can be learned, but that's only because I've been trying
for twenty years and I still haven't got the knack.

There are cracks in my resumé as large as a lifetime—
and no one wants to hear about motherhood
as a transferable skill. I attend a well-being seminar
on resilience, and I take note of the other mothers
in the room. We have lived through worse than this.

[BEEP]

Mum comes to visit, and we argue about the capital
gains tax in the car from the airport. It's not that we've
run out of things to fight about, we just pick the most
topical. Like most people her age, she thinks that they
worked harder for their money back in the day. Of course
she's also tricked me into taking leave to pick her up
because she can't figure out the bus. She's bought
the cheapest flights, right on rush hour, and we are stuck.
On goes the radio to turn off our fight, and someone
is in the middle of saying, *Women are subsidising
the capitalist economy with their unpaid labour*, and
for once we are both speechless with agreement.

[BEEP]

Mostly I'm dire with memory of a childhood
when the solemn tune of Mr Whippy seemed
to bring with it a memory from a past life
in a cold-river country where I learned to sing
in another language. But that was only yesterday, or
last week, when I skinned my knees falling from my
orange pogo stick. Summers went on so long our hair
turned green from the school pool and matted from the sea.
We were creatures out of time and I don't know
when I'll have that luxury again.

[BEEP]

What if there was time for each friend's face, glowing
with warm recognition as we meet in the lilac evening—
discussing where to go for dinner, who has the best
desserts, who the vegan wine list, what we *feel* like. What if
we had time to look up, to ride the weather, to play
with our children and to call our sisters for a proper talk
for once. What would happen if I stopped running from thing
to thing and walked for a moment, directionless.

Love poem as women's work

There are so many tiny hitches, every day. I wake up and think, God, I have to wash my hair. And you know how that goes—I block the plughole again. Again, I check my breasts for lumps with conditioner running down my back. Amazing how I am destined to find what I'm looking for. My horoscope app tells me I can be a world unto myself, and I find that I already am.

Stopping in for two-for-one Tuesdays at the video store after doing the grocery shopping. Checking out something black-and-white and something for the kids, because we couldn't afford the new release rack. What did we do before we binge-watched television? Everything was analogue then, the evenings ticking neatly to their closure. Just getting the children to bed seemed to take all night.

A blackbird flies into the window and lies twitching on the ground outside for several minutes as we watch from behind the glass. Next day it happens again. I sigh and take up the shovel. I try to forget that we live in a country of fitfully dozing volcanoes. Any of them could wake, any minute. My nails are always catching on something as I stride out into the fault.

Sometimes I find myself looking at my children, nearly taller than me now, and thinking, I will be survived by them. Sometimes I find myself looking at the man I made them with and thinking, will we survive the raising of them.

Serial killer glasses

I get them from the 'Skandi' section at Specsavers—it's buy one, get one free, so I take a risk. It's only later, when a friend forwards me a link to serial killers' mugshots, that I see it. Even the Zodiac, supposedly, had them—on the Wanted poster, his eyes glare out from under squarish wire rims. Every pair of glasses I've owned till now has been tortoiseshell and round. Librarian glasses. Well, it's true, branding never hurts, and they do look cute with a cardigan and a tweed skirt. When I started work at the library, there was a rumour of a book bound in human skin, kept in the rare books cage. Being a librarian, I did my research. I learnt how to tell the difference between calf-skin and sheep-skin binding—that human-skin binding is most often mistaken for pig. I read about the treatise on female virginity bound in the skin of an unknown woman, embossed delicately with gold leaf. How the owner would carry it round with him, pull it out at parties. I was nearly disappointed that our book was only a rumour, even though I wouldn't have been able to touch it—I can't even cut raw chicken without using a fork to steady the breast against the knife. Can't bear the fridge-cold flesh against my fingers. Paring out the bloody bits. The gristle and fat. Horrified by it. Right until it touches my lips.

Bad man kink

Three days later and you are still
a bad man. A bad man but my smell
is on you now like ash on the exhale
of the world burning.

I'm bad at sleeping with you—expelling
you from my bed at 2am, I lock the door
behind you before your Uber even arrives—
let you blind your way down my path
in the dark.

I think it's probably good for you
to be put out like this, an animal
into the night, and it's good
for me too—I need the sleep, but

I don't sleep well—I dream of a smiling man
with a bomb strapped to his chest
arriving at my work. I wake
and the fear is working my heart
so hard it almost feels like desire.

The next time
I see you, I'm protesting
outside Parliament and you walk past
with your swipe card, a new tattoo
under your shirt sleeve.

You pretend you're protesting too
but you have little interest in women's
reproductive rights. And even less

knowledge of body politics.
Three months and your spell
is still on me, you say, a little afraid
because I like to play
the witch. You buy me

lunch, and I bring my placard
with me. CAN'T TOUCH THIS
it declares in rainbow lettering, and I can
tell you're worried you'll be seen
by someone who matters.

There is a kink for cishet
white men, but I don't think I have it.

The first time you cooked for me
you described the meal
by its ingredients, and I could tell
they were expensive.

But you don't have the knack—
what I call the *easy hand*—
no matter how much you'd like to think
of yourself as a Renaissance man.

Later, I lie in your bathtub
eating an apricot, lush flesh lifting
easily from the toxic core, as
you exalt your marble tiles

and I imagine holding you down
face-first in the water
between my legs.

Like us

Towards the end, when we kissed I was thinking less of your lips
and more of the great Russian novels—Levin scything rhythmically.
The corsets and velvets, the long, blue wind.

Our kisses weren't like that, and nothing ever is.

Symbolically, our houseplants developed brown stains on their leaves
that year and slowly stopped growing. The walls were pathological.
Clean clothes from the wardrobe smelled like wet dirt.
There were things about you that I couldn't live with.

One of your great-grandfathers raped and killed his infant
daughter, then boiled and ate her flesh. You kept a photo of him
on our wall, and I looked the other direction every time I walked past.

One day I stopped letting you tie me to the bed,
and when you asked why, I didn't trust you enough to tell you
it was because I didn't trust you. I still don't.

If you are reading this it's because I'm dead.
Or maybe you're dead, looking over my shoulder from elsewhere
while 'Ignition (Remix)' plays in the background. Like that time
the bouncer called me 'your slut', and I cried in the bathroom
and you continued to dance without me, the green and purple light
shimmering off your face.

It's true we're both terrible in our incompatible ways.

The day I finally walked out I threw myself into an internet
wormhole of unsolved murders. I became my own lady detective—
never looking back when I walk home at night, never without

a knife. The ghosts of dead women whirlpool around me
dragging the heads of their murderers by their hair.

What I can tell you is this: most of the time it isn't a criminally insane man
with his blood turning to dust in his veins, walking through
an unlocked door and unzipping a person from their body like a coat.
Most of the time it is a person you love.

You said that the only thing worth remembering is that Vronsky shoots
his beloved horse. He so desperately wants to win the race that he whips
it until its body breaks beneath him. Anna says his name, and the whole world
knows she loves him. Just like anyone who's ever loved anyone gives it away
in the saying of their name.

That's where I stopped reading. The tragic demise of their love
and Anna in front of the train were only ruined for me when you said
But that's the one thing everyone knows about Anna Karenina!

But no one ever read those books in my house, and no one knew
they were meant to. Turns out knowledge is a class war that you keep winning.
Really, what's the point? Surely, the moral of this whole, great book
is exactly that there is no point?

Like us walking through the park in autumn, the air full
of the brewery's smell of Weet Bix and warm milk,
our hands swinging, intertwined, between us.

Like us reading from either end of the couch, our legs
meeting in the middle.

Like when you text to say *I miss you*
and my insides churn like the creek full of eels
under our torchlight. Goddamn you.
Like us.

Seahorses

I'm walking along the waterfront
listening to a podcast about telepathy
when I see an ex with her new partner
and their small daughter

who has the same wispy white curls
that my own daughter used to have
sixteen years ago, tied adorably
in a fountain on the top of her head

and who is insisting that she has seen
a seahorse. My ex, in an expensive
camel coat and the same perfume
she used to wear obscuring the fresh-fish
smell of the harbour

keeps responding, *No seahorses
in there*, and I'm reminded how plainly
literal she always was. How bad
the role-play, how unsurprising
the dates. How she thought

we should stop seeing each other
because she hadn't imagined
herself spending so much time
around children.

All week there have been record
rains, and the harbour is scummy
round the edges, but full and green
in its depths. She catches my eye

and I will her not to say hello, not to
introduce me to her wife and child, not
to draw me in. But she's the kind
of woman who could never
get a sense for the unsaid.

They talk about their private-sector
jobs and how difficult it is to find
good childcare and I wonder if she
feels the same as she used to

about Anthony Bourdain, now that he is dead.
The inferior celebrity chef, she thought,
preferring the blonde exuberance
of Jamie Oliver, who 'actually cooks'.

I make an excuse as their daughter
declares, again, that she has seen
a seahorse. But I can't help myself—
Yes, I say, *I saw it too.*

Not the friendly shape of a seahorse—
but a stingray. Unmistakable dark
shadow moving below the surface
exactly where she was pointing.

She'd got one word wrong and so
they hadn't even looked.
That's how it goes sometimes—
everything depends on the one thing
you're not sure about.

Thought experiment in the future

When I was a kid watching *The Jetsons*
on Saturday morning, I assumed
we'd have flying cars by now, and robots
to do our work.

Instead, I'm in a long-distance
relationship with consolation.

There is so little power in knowing
the future, now that I'm in it. How many palms
must I read before I see something
akin to hope?

I walk to the wind turbines and am amazed
at how like walking through a forest it is—
machines aspirating like enormous trees

and I can't help but look up, pressing my face
to the sun with the primordial intuition
of alive things.

But unlike a forest, this is not a place
where a human might seek shelter.

There is no undergrowth; no lizards
twitch from my shadow. Just brown grass
shorn close.

Still afraid of the dark

Back when I was living alone,
I would draw all the curtains and turn
on all the lights as the dark came down.
If I arrived home after nightfall, I would run
from room to room checking behind all the doors
and inside all the wardrobes! And why? Those
are the very places darkness is!
Now, of course, I am not so silly. I live with
my family and I am nearly certain that the dark
can't get me with all this colour and warmth
and noise—oh, it's an evolutionary trick—the dark
can't get me with all this light around.

Who doesn't love miniature horses

Since reading about the gut-brain axis I've been tending my microbiome with a cult-like intensity. That is to say, the intensity of a boomer couple who've retired to a lifestyle block to grow microgreens and weed and maybe breed some miniature horses to entertain the grandkids. Because who doesn't love miniature horses? I love miniature horses, and I love them more when I'm not depressed. I tend my gut flora with kefir and prebiotics, with kombucha and yoghurt. If I can *just* fix the balance of bacteria on my insides, who knows what else I might love? It's easier to strive for gut health than to strive for *happiness*, because it feels like the more we strive for happiness, the less of it there is to get. When I say 'we', I mean 'me and my friends'—this poetry business is all so anecdotal. Our parents left us to be baby-sat by existential anime and games where we controlled speeding neon worlds. Our homework was times tables and *What do you want to be when you grow up?* because back then we could be anything. But we were nine years old—how could we possibly know? *We just want you to be happy,* our parents boomed. And happiness was a cartoon sun at the end of a rainbow. It shone with the promise of a good job, a good house, a nuclear family, a golden retriever, a vege patch. And we're nearly blind from looking at it directly, because if we turn away we'll see that we'll never own our own homes. And there's an island of garbage in the Pacific. And the rainforest is shrinking. And we're paying for our parents' retirements, their funerals, their mistakes. And we're broken on the inside.

Love poem on Valentine's Day

Sorry to be so sappy, but you're the one who made us
take the 'love languages' quiz online and validated my greed
for gifts. Your result said you respond best to 'words of love'
and psshh, I thought, easy, I am a poet, after all. Now here I am
on the day, wondering if it's too late to buy some frilly knickers
and a new sex toy instead. Is it? How many times have I told you
I love you, do you think? In rapt pleasure, or just after, or as you
pull a bottle of wine from the grocery bags like a kind-hearted
magician? Parting on our way to work all those mornings, oh
shall I count the ways? Believe me, if there was a better way
to say it than this, I would. Not that I want to hold your hands
in front of a crowd and declare anything—you know that'd
make me cry. But I do want you to know that I'd like to keep
spending time with you . . . till we both get old and die.

The World

for Joy

It is the ball of wool originally spun by the mother
goddess from her own dark hair—unravelling like currency

It is the fourth belly of the bronze cow tended by the
lowborn prophet—eking the last nutrients from waste

A tooth loosened from the gum of God and dropped
wishless—bloody black hole plugged by a giant tongue

*

It is a broken bone healed badly—the whole
body grown crooked around it

The stent in the heart of childhood friends, now
corporate rivals who hack at a golf ball in the sand

A phlegmatic death rattle like mud in a vaulted church—
no amount of incense, no holy mothers can clear it

*

It has all the symptoms of a middle child—dramatically
failing in school just to get a bit of attention

It's the cool uncle selling cocaine overseas—his pinky
finger mailed home, still wearing the tourmaline signet ring

It's the bride at a mass wedding—less interesting than all the
other girls orbiting round an ugly but charismatic man

*

It's the everlasting gobstopper changing colours every
few centuries—cracked in two by a strong-jawed giant

The medieval version of a turducken—a lark inside a quail
all the way out to a peacock with its tail sewn back on

The royal family carving through the dripping meaty
layers while peasants starve in the fields

*

It's an Easter egg hunt, but all the eggs are real eggs
instead of chocolate, and they're rotten

The fussy Victorian valentine bought online—
painted with the arsenic that will eventually kill you

The quietest float in the Christmas parade—no lolly
scramble, no Irish dancers—just bursting into flames

*

It's a battlefield for the gods—how we keep fighting over
them like there's a single answer to the question of belief

It's Time closing her throat against the bitter music rising
there—all the history she will not sing

It's love like the lustre on the ceramic bowl you inherited
from your mother—and it will not break and it will not break

*

Everything we think we know is through lived experience
only—there is no scientific method for a life

It is the illusion of choice for a future where we swim with
our friends in water as bluegreenwhite as the earth from space

and the caterpillars leave, for once, our tomato plants to ripen
and the world turns on an axis of milky benevolence

With careful hand

First, the tan spider travelling indoors on the hem
of my long black skirt, taken out to the garden
and released under the lemon tree.

Then, the worm writhing on the drying footpath
ferried carefully to a patch of muddy grass.

But then, horror, the glass snail, still translucent
and soft, thrown from my shower door as I step in.

I scoop it up in toilet paper and flush it away.
Too late to carry it outside to the daffodils
to do its hungry devastation there.

Some days are so long that I have no kindness
in me and then, when I do, I have a killer's hands.

Libraries like icebergs

Proximity to the library is having one's hand on the pulse of the universe. It's turning to see a dear friend in a room absolutely rotten with strangers. It's looking down on a familiar city from a great height, sweat cooling on your back, and it's still, so still, that you might've missed the apocalypse. It's the streetlight blinking when you walk below it, a small owl calling from the bush beyond the fence. It's that barometric lift of understanding when thoughts move like weather, like emotion. It's the feeling of extreme up-closeness that comes from finding out more, and then more again, about the person you love. The secret dimness of the backstage. It's the feeling I had as a child reading *The Borrowers*, imagining the whole world in cross-sectioned miniature—that's how I see the library—like a doll's house, hinged open at its heart, tiny readers bent over tiny books. Being inside the library is like flying inside a cloud—shut off from the outside, riding out its knocks and bumps. Libraries, like mushrooms all connected underground, like hibernation, like glimpsing the glittering elbow of a gem poking out of dark rock. Libraries, like icebergs, balancing out the seen with the great unseen, all that knowledge stacked below the surface, keeping us all afloat. Libraries, like icebergs, disappearing.

Finally, I might be getting somewhere

for Always

I am a pinecone. Which is like a flower but better, like a fruit but bitter, like a seed but bigger. I am full of seeds, which means I'm full of myself. I'm what they mean when they say *Has Potential*. Some of my relatives are thousands of years old and convey reports of comets and the deep parts of the earth. Some of them are turned into frames for windows that look onto treeless gardens, for doors that look over the ocean, for paintings of the old revolutions. Some of them are turned into flames. Wind from the south this morning and it was the scratching of an audience in a gilded theatre before the chinning of the violins. You will note that I haven't yet learned the trick of describing myself without comparing myself to others, but I have learned the trick of the wind. I know about hanging on. For years I've been practising falling, without ever letting go. For years I've been practising waiting in the dark on the forest floor with my mouth shut. When I speak, it will be a tree.

Chauvet Cave

It's 30,000 years ago   and you are already ripe with ceremonial magic.
I come to you to make marks on you   to leave *my* mark on you. I record
      my conquests on your skin—the bison I hunted, the mammoth
            but you are the unconquerable.

                                        *

            It's 5000 years later and you haven't aged a bit. I come in
from the glaciers and light my fire among the bones of animals
      I've never seen in the flesh   but which are painted on
your flanks. Through the smoke of my fire past my shadow
      rearing up on the walls   as the flames bloom
the animals stalk me.   I do not sleep easy here.
            *   *

            It's 1994, and I've just discovered you. I'll give
      you my name, and you'll become famous—
respectable. But for now, wow, you are wild and so lonely.
      It's been 10,000 years since you heard the voice of a human,
            the spirits of the animals in your skin braying and fraying
and running loud. Seeing you by electric light domesticates
            you and for our return I suggest candles, torches,
      a campfire, but the heat is dangerous.   They say
                              the heat will destroy you.
                                          * *   *

You are Chauvet Cave   and I'm an entirely new branch
      of science   dedicated only to you. I want to understand you
gateway   gatekeeper   other side   your altar cradling
      the skull of a prehistoric human. The rocky column
      where a woman's painted legs and vulva blend into
a bison's head. I want to understand   the ritual of getting
      closer to you   the red handprints slapping against you
            slapping against the spirit world.
                  I need to know if they broke through.
            *   *   *   *

64

You are Chauvet Cave   and I'm Werner Herzog   wearing sterile boots
and something like covetousness in my mullioned insect eyes.
I interview you   without touching you.   Inside you, I do not once rest my
hand against you but I can feel you   yearning. I know you're trying
   to tell me something   which I must communicate with the world, and I
   ask the team for silence.   Later, when I put the film together
            I dub over this with cello and viola   trying to capture something
            something of what I heard.

           **   *   *   *

      You are Chauvet Cave   and I'm watching you   at home
      without the aid of 3D glasses. Herzog gestures   to you and says
      that you are decorated only in your darkest   most secret parts.
      The French archaeologist   who used to be in the circus
            turns away from his bulky grey laptop and describes
            the first week of visiting you daily. *It was too much,*
            he says. *I was dreaming of lions.*   Werner asks if they
            were real or painted.   *Real,* he replies, *but I was not
            afraid.*   The camera pans slowly over the skull
            of a cave bear turned porcelain.   Thousands of years
            of slow sculpture.   Your patience   your art.

         *   *   *   *   *

      You are Chauvet Cave and I've come to visit you in person.
   But you are not   yourself.   Scientists have mapped every
      millimetre of you with laser scanners   and reproduced you.
      Everything is exact—   the temperature   the humidity
      the silence.   Even the smell   designed in a Parisian atelier.
   But the hairs   refuse   to rise   along the back of my neck.
I want to slap my hands   against your walls   like the old humans,
pigment squelching between my fingers. This is what I came here
for—to look at the past from the inside.   To slip out of my
      humanity like clothes   and raise my hands in glory
      or surrender

Grandiflora

Big-top of a tree in my grandparents' backyard.
This is where I pitch myself, with my book

and my box of Heards barley sugars, after
five hours squashed in the back seat of the car.

Under the leaves like waxy green rosettes—
the flowers meaty and pale pink as cupped hands

emitting the lemony fragrance of Sunlight dish soap.
The murky veil of quiet as the world buzzes outside.

Sky always some variation on grey—chinoiserie
wallpaper in silver foil. White pepper and papyrus.

Moonstone, agate, lead. A different sky to home—
an inland sky. Windless and stale with chimney smoke.

At the funeral, a story I've never heard before—
my grandparents camping beneath the tree on hot nights.

Back when it was safe to sleep with doors
unlocked, my aunts and uncles quiet in their cots.

Nostalgia flares like memory, not my own, but close.
Tender generational yearning for a past I cannot have.

I should be looking hopefully down the barrel
of this long century. Looking hopefully ahead.

The way my grandparents would walk to the end
of the driveway to wave us off. Then just my grandfather.

Then, last time we visited, no one to wave goodbye to
when we left. And no one to come back for at all

except this, the largest tree of its kind in the whole
southern hemisphere. So ancient it existed before

bees, its flowers pollinated by flying beetles instead.
Our whole family history tucked safely under.

OMG, am I a hedonist?

Drinking from an art deco crystal champagne
coupe with a hollow stem is a commitment
to understanding a different kind of lived

experience to my own. In some ways I feel
oh, even more contemporary when I do this—
with my nail polish that can detect a spiked drink.

I could so easily have been born in the wrong
time. God, it is hell to even think of it. If I
went back to then, my eyeshadow alone

would give me away. But I am planted in my own
time like a tree with many leaves and no
fruits. No fruits yet, but damn I can feel them

coming. I'm not a sensual person, I wouldn't
have said, but I do like to be touched . . .
yes, like that. I am absolutely here for this—

the way you oh-so-lightly tap me on the ass
like you're still not sure if this is something
people do. Propping myself up on one elbow

in your bed, each kiss is a white lie, but there
is nothing so sexy as reassurance and a silk
pillowcase. Do you, too, remember with

fondness the craze for body chocolate
in the early 2000s? God, the absolute
charmlessness of that time, when all I had

going for me was my youth and horniness.
Each day is a canyon of light that I must
press myself into or be forgotten forever.

Do you feel this way too? Okay, I admit
when we watch the eclipse of the blood moon
your arms around me feel like the origin

of the universe. Stars crackling their primal static.
Your breath in my hair the first time anyone
has done this. You are wearing a perfume

that is supposed to smell like lightning
in the aurora borealis and I am so grateful to you
for not choosing something basic on the nose.

All I want is another pair of earrings and
a deep emotional connection with someone
I enjoy fucking, is that too much to ask?

I want only treasure, I don't want all the other
junk. OMG, am I a hedonist, I wonder, and
is there an elegant way to eat slivers of raw fish?

I always feel so wrong in my body, especially
if someone is looking at me. And this is why,
you know, I wear the most ridiculous dresses.

Semi-final in Scorpio season

Three moons into the season and I'm walking down Cuba Street
to meet a friend. Singing yawns from a distance, and I mistake
it for Christmas carols. Five steps closer and—the young men
gathered at the mouth of the bar, some with fists
to their hearts. The national anthem, my most dreaded form of PDA.

Upstairs, the gig fumbles me in its current the way I allow myself
to be swooshed in deep water—the only thing I ever give in to.
I nearly forget my body, furious, and enjoying it
behind a young woman whose hair keeps flicking my face—
her arms raised and head down, properly in it.

My friend shout-whispers into my ear, *Remember
the first time we saw them, lying on the floor
of Aro Valley Community Centre?* I do, her voice slips
down my spine and settles heavy in the small of my back.

I remember the music doing the work of tearing out
my pulpy heart, licking it clean, and pressing it back into my chest.
I remember us sitting outside on the park bench drinking fire
from a hipflask and talking to the whole city as it walked home.

I remember feeling different, and wanting a mirror to see myself in—
tender and repaired, but settling for a selfie
where I looked right into my own eyes
instead of away, like I usually do.

Waiting in line for the toilet between bands
someone says to me, *You're the poet*, and I want to deny it.
I feel caught out, guilty for being a person

who considers the world a lot, but is no good at making any noise
about it, and busting.

It's only when I catch an Uber home that I discover
we've lost at the thing we're supposed to do best.
My driver says his friend, a medium, told him we'd lose
earlier this week. His angel cards too, but he didn't want to believe it.

Everything is slicked holographic in the sudden rain
and the street is the ozone scent of river water
moving fast over rock. I don't say
I might've watched if I'd known we'd lose.

Hags

Simple to pass through the world
as an invisible woman—more complicated, though
easier, as a beautiful one.

I only realised this when I stopped
being beautiful, age sliding over me like
an old-timey nightgown, ghosting me.

I say this from the softly potent age of thirty-three—
a crone in a tower poring over past years
like lovers. Oh, that one was blond and dry-hot

and smelt like cardamom and honey.
That one was darker, edges opaque
and grimed with the bad drugs.

Life has left its pockmarks on me already
but has done it so gradually I haven't mourned.
My daughter even, her rose face

pimpled over, the scars of small accidents
recorded only in her skin:
a burn mark on her left inner wrist—

the gash in her forehead from being hit
with a wooden block by another kid
at preschool.

This is how we die, if we're lucky, by degrees—
our participation dependant on being seen
till we're not. I've never met a woman

who isn't striving for another way to look.
The restless reinvention of clothes and make-up,
the hope of a new haircut.

We're thinking women, obviously; we know
about Le Corbusier, and the lunar eclipse,
and the stalking of Theresa Saldana

but that doesn't mean we're not susceptible
to the trappings of our bodies, strange in a new dress.
The effect of a new medication on our skin.

The way we don't want to be seen
to be trying too hard. *Look at me!* we cry.
Over here! Look me in the eyes.

Butch era

One perfect pair of new trousers
and suddenly I'm in charge.
Leaning confidently against the bar
with my arms crossed, tattoos sprouting
across my biceps, flirting with the
bartender while she shakes
me up a whisky cocktail.

Cats flock to me, and women too,
sensing something amiss. That old
shrinking self, gone. And in its place,
well, you tell me—my skin is clear
and my hands are strong. I develop
a little swagger, a Clea DuVall glint
in my eye. I sleep unselfconsciously
in a different bed each night.

My friends ask what's different.
I'm in my butch era, I reply.
And my phone auto-corrects *butch*
to *bitch*, but hey, I don't care, I'm busy
fighting the final boss of the imperialist
white supremacist heteropatriarchy.
I wear the trousers now, I just might win.

Coven

Unsleeping in the dark, I count my friends
for reassurance, rather than sheep.
I turn to them like the dog-eared pages
of a favourite book. Each with their own
reliquaries of chaos and glory.

They found me haphazardly—
I never sought them out, never asked
the schoolyard question *Will you be my friend*
and yet here we are with our pre-Raphaelite
hair and our tiger's claw earrings

and our difficult backstories.
The relief of them—the relief
of not knowing, together, quite the right way
to prepare an artichoke or gut a fish
or talk to our parents.

Side hustle as an alchemist

A few years shy of mid-life and planning my crises
because who knows how long a life will be, and so
who knows where the middle is. The obvious choice
is to get into brewing, like all the cool dads with scrubby
beards and a couple of tattoos. Except, being handier
in the kitchen, I'll be brewing the elixir of life.

Cynic that I am, I know there's no point dragging out
the big soup pot till I've got my head in order. I offer
jealousy back to all those who have given it to me. I hoick
my grudges into expectant hands. I joke to ease the awkwardness—
Don't use it all at once, ha! I've never been a big talker—
just practising spells under my breath every once in a while.

Spells, jokes, poems—same, same. I can be
very articulate for short periods of time, so what?
The base, as we know, is coffee, chartreuse and cherry cola—
but the other bits and pieces I'm having mailed in.
A level of organisation that is very out of character, I admit—
but so is living forever. I'm just trying to do it right.

Those monks told us the recipe, but they were
speaking Italian and I didn't understand. Probably
for the best, one less bit of unlearning to be done.
I like the idea of it—ruby, gold and pearl ground up
with jasmine oil and snail mucin. Top shelf stuff, but too easy
to get a hold of. In goes the milky reflux of my babies instead.

In goes my first copy of Noel Streatfeild's *Ballet Shoes*.
In goes everyone I've ever made read it—i.e. everyone
I've ever loved. In goes the bath bomb called 'Goddess'—

galactic purple and sparkling so that for an hour or two I can
be a woman glittering at the centre of everything. I have to remind
myself that what I'm *not* doing is packing for the afterlife.

Otherwise I'd be needing a sarcophagus, one of those fancy
ones, punctured with glory holes and painted with gold—
and I can't afford the freight on that. What I can afford
is eternal youth. At least, what I'm willing to pay for is
a pink clay face mask and Maybelline waterproof mascara
from the toiletries aisle at the supermarket. They go in.

Look at me, I paint my self-portrait every morning
in the mirror. My motivations are pure, though I'm still
searching for meaning. Still searching for my Chapstick in
a last-ditch way every time I leave the house. Time
is a construct, and yet I am always late. Bus gliding
away like a swan on the varnished surface of a slow river.

Swans go in, and buses! Orange tulips in cellophane.
FIMO necklace with dolphins riding high on the curl of a wave.
Diorama of the sphinx at the provincial museum. The way
I felt the first time I heard Shania Twain say *Let's go girls*.
In goes Shania. In goes leopard print. In goes the hipflask
with my grandmother's lipstick still on the rim.

That sounds dirty, and it is. Dirt goes in, and my grannies,
both of them, because they knew how to live. And what
would they have to say about all of this, keeping an eye
on me from the other side? Remembering when driving too fast
on the open road was the only way to wick their rage.
Cranking the stove up hot, *Come on, then, get on with it*.

The water

I'm devastated by this lack—
but language does not come—
I keep thinking, if I could go back—

my hand on your arm as you boarded, stay with me today—
our stories would have been of luck gleaming sweetly—

like the morning after a familiar dream—
instead, a long keening and black—
headlong into thickets of storm—

daily I ask the water this question—
daily it turns its back

Vantablack

I want to sleep but I am thinking about their shoes
left at the entrance, the rising water—
the incomprehensible chambers, the hungry

air pockets within. Every bit of footage looks like an ultrasound—
something fluttering and tentative—the dense mountain
pressing down.

It's so dark that they don't know when to sleep or to wake up—
that the world is hanging loosely off the periphery
of their lantern.

To be looked at, to be looked for, gives the illusion of safety—
nothing can go wrong when someone is watching.
Which is why, I suppose, people believe in God.

In lieu of prayer, I open a book and a book-shaped void appears
in my hands. The pavilion at the Winter Olympics painted
in Vantablack and illuminated by a million LED stars.

Double-spread pages show the building's negative silhouette
against a pale blue sky, but my favourite is the one with the snowy
mountains of Pyeongchang in the background—

a crane, some ugly modern townhouses.
Surely a hole punched through the fabric of reality
is never punched somewhere picturesque.

If this was a real black hole we would already have been
eaten alive. Instead, the first group of boys emerges from the cave—
blinking in the light of the world's attention.

Poem while watching the world burn

Head glittering with a hangover, I step outside into air fuggy with ash—
the sun a small red hole burnt through by a curious god
with a magnifying glass.

A man approaches me on the street with a handful of leaflets, proclaims
This is how the world ends!

What it might've been like if we didn't live in times when news
travels faster than weather.
On the television, footage of the fires from space—
the long drag of smoke over the water.

But the sunsets, the news anchor says, *are like nothing you've ever seen.*
The past keeps its old grammar, the comfortable construction of it.
Of the future—it is a sentence with too many syllables—
we avoid speaking it.

I drive as far as this country can take me—
to where the two oceans meet and the land runs out, just to see some water.
I had thought it would be as calm as traffic merging downtown—
this place where souls leap into the afterlife.

Instead, two oceans of different colours are pulled apart by warring moons.
For the first time in my life, I can't regulate my breath by the waves.

*

Then, advancing like an enemy army, the virus comes.
Hiding in our homes, we hope it'll pass over our lintels and leave us—
taking its shades, the melodramatic odour of the season, with it.

It seems like we have been walking forever
within the minefields of our bodies.
Keeping our breath close and our hands clean.

*

Then religion comes knocking—a one-two punch in a neat suit.
Religion comes, knocking back the bright decades of progress.
Knocking us up and leaving us for dead.

The fires are coming from further afield now, but we feel, more
and more, the heat from them. For example, I'm still liable for my womb.
I'm still burning inside my skin.

*

If only the earth was a brain that could rinse herself clean as we sleep.
Really, there is no ultimatum we might offer except our own extinction.

Maybe what happened is this—we searched hard for a word to convey
that what is gone is gone forever, and lady earth earned it.

So we did what we do with everything good—
we poured on some petrol, lit a match
and we burned it.

After the party, the new year

Guests will begin arriving soon, and I should
be vacuuming the floor, mixing the punch.
Instead, I'm polishing my mirror.

A full-length thing with a rounded top.
I polish till it's so bright it looks like a door
cut from the coat-tails of the moon.

I want this to be the first thing my friends see
when they arrive. To see themselves stepping
into an archway of gleaming light as if into a new
and good year.

After the party, the potato chips ground into
the carpet, the stale slices of baguette, the fingerprints
of a small child drawn in enthusiastic abstract
through the centre of the mirror.

The day overcast and solemn with everything
we said and hoped at midnight.
The new year tender as a bud.

Notes

The title poem, 'Saga' (p. 11) was written in response to Mary Ruefle's poem 'Saga', from *Trances of the Blast* (Wave Books, 2013). This is also where the book's epigraph comes from.

'Praying the gay away' (p. 20) is structured around the classic 'five stages of grief': denial, anger, bargaining, depression and acceptance.

'Bury your queers' (p. 22) is named for the trope in which queer characters in film, television and literature are far more likely to die than their non-queer counterparts. The poem specifically refers to the death of Tara in *Buffy the Vampire Slayer*.

'La bohème' (p. 23) takes its title and general jumping-off point (a poor artist and her poor friends) from the Puccini opera of the same name.

'Three times a cat lady' (p. 28) takes its title from the song 'Three times a lady' by the Commodores, from the album *Natural High* (Motown, 1978).

'The well of loneliness' (p. 36) is based on the novel of the same name by Radclyffe Hall. The so-called 'lesbian bible' was subject to an obscenity trial following its publication in 1928, which made me think it'd be juicy, but it is, in fact, a very boring book, imho. Radclyffe Hall sounds like an awful person: from all accounts she was a racist, anti-Semitic, fascist, anti-radical pro-Eugenicist. I quite enjoyed killing her off (via Stephen), although it has to be acknowledged that this book paved the way for much of the queer literature I know and love.

'Beep test' (p. 41) references Kim Hill's interview with Dr Kristen Ghodsee about her book *Why Women Have Better Sex Under Socialism* (Vintage, 2018) on Radio New Zealand, 12 April 2020.

'Serial killer glasses' (p. 47) mentions the 17th-century book on female virginity bound in human skin by Dr Ludovic Bouland around 1865. He is thought to have acquired the skin from the body of an unknown woman who died in hospital when Bouland was a medical student.

'Like us' (p. 50) references Tolstoy's *Anna Karenina* and the serial killer Richard Chase.

'Love poem on Valentine's Day' (p. 57) draws on Elizabeth Barrett Browning's iconic *Sonnets from the Portuguese* (1850) and references, in particular, sonnet 43, 'How do I love thee?'

'With careful hand' (p. 61) borrows from Fleur Adcock's poem 'For a Five-Year-Old', *Poems, 1960–2000* (Bloodaxe Books, 2000).

'Chauvet Cave' (p. 64) was written after watching Werner Herzog's documentary *Cave of Forgotten Dreams* (2010).

'Butch era' (p. 74) uses bell hooks' succinct and damning term for the systems which bind us, the 'imperialist white supremacist heteropatriarchy'.

'Vantablack' (p. 79) refers to the 2018 rescue of the junior association football team who became trapped in the Tham Luang Nang Non cave in Chiang Rai Province, northern Thailand. As I was trying to imagine how dark it must've been in the cave, at work I began to catalogue a book about Vantablack, the 'world's darkest material', supposedly absorbing up to 99% of visible light.

The final lines of 'Poem while watching the world burn' (p. 80) riff on the final lines of Eavan Boland's poem 'Atlantis—A Lost Sonnet', *Domestic Violence* (W. W. Norton, 2007).

Acknowledgements

Always, thanks to my sister witches and writing heroes: Magnolia and Morgan, you are truly the best coven a gal could have! With extra thanks to Morgs, for daring me to send this in before I believed it was a book, and for being my 'poetry club of one' for a year or so: I'm so lucky to be launching with you. 🖤

Thanks to writing clubs of years past and present: Morgan (again), Magnolia, Therese, Emma and Ash for reading these in bits. Funny now to think of each hard-won poem being wrangled into decency with the help of your incredible hearts and brains!

Thanks a thousand times to Fran for being my best 'artist-but-not-a-writer' friend, I love talking craft and chaos and cheese with you. Thanks for all the games of Bananagrams and gallery visits. These poems aren't as sparkly as your jewels, but I hope you can see your influence!

Thanks to Poetry Pals for the enthusiasm and community, and for helping me to love poetry again.

To the GLAM group, Audrey, Lillie, Terence, Richard and Miranda, for making work bearable and life nice, and for letting me join the gang even though I'm neither young nor professional. Especially thanks to Audrey and Terence for supporting me through my butch era and for alllll the yum cha.

Thanks to Stef, for being an absolute icon and legend, and showing me that it's possible to have a professional life even if you feel like a out-of-place space-cadet poet at times. And for sending me those serial killers' mugshots!

Thanks to Always and Joy for commissioning poems that appear in this book. It was such an honour to be asked (I love and admire both your work so much), especially when I was in my 'can't write' phase. These poems helped shake me out of my funk, and I'm forever grateful.

Thanks to the Brills for all your wisdom and support over the years; I'm so lucky to bask in the presence of such brilliant and amazing writers and mothers. Thanks for helping me figure out that one particular poem.

Thanks to Fergus for agreeing to do this a second time. Thanks to Ashleigh for believing in my silly poems and not letting me take them all out. Bless you for making it seem as though I know how grammar and punctuation work. Thanks to Andy for the pastel psychedelic cover of my dreams and to Ebony for your generous, genius eye. Many kisses of gratitude to Rebecca (and Morgan, AGAIN) for saying such nice things for the cover.

Thanks to the Margaret King Spencer Writers Encouragement Trust for funding me to write in Italy for a month. What a dream. Some of those poems appear in this book.

Thanks to the editors and journals who've published many of these poems over the years—especially Paula Green at *NZ Poetry Shelf*, Chris Tse at *The Spinoff*, Rebecca and Nikki-Lee at *Sweet Mammalian*, and Grace at *Overcom*.

Thanks, most of all, to Minsa, Gewlga and Kimmoo: creative consultant, aesthetic advisor and patron of the arts. Thanks for cheerleading me to do this absolutely nuts and pointless thing that I do. And to Waffles, most loyal lad, muse and one true love.